THINK HAPPY,
BE HAPPY

Library of Congress Cataloging-in-Publication Data is available.

ISBN 978-0-7611-7757-9

Workman books are available at special discounts when purchased
in bulk for premiums and sales promotions as well as for
fund-raising or educational use. Special editions or book excerpts
can also be created to specification. For details, contact the
Special Sales Director at the address below or
send an email to specialsales@workman.com.

Design by Netta Rabin

Cover and title page illustration © Jessie Schneider

Workman Publishing Co., Inc.
225 Varick Street
New York, NY 10014-4381
workman.com

WORKMAN is a registered trademark of Workman Publishing Co., Inc.

Printed in China
First printing October 2013

10 9 8

THINK HAPPY,
BE HAPPY

art, inspiration, joy

Workman Publishing • New York

Happy Little
A^INTRODUCTION

Feel the sunshine.

Lift your spirits.

Dream big dreams . . .
and some little ones, too.

Think happy.

Be happy.

A 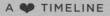 TIMELINE

10,000 BCE: The heart symbol is first used by Cro-Magnon hunters.

15th century: The first modern deck of playing cards features the heart as a mark of one of the red suits.

18th century: The heart becomes an icon of love, beauty, purity, and wisdom among African nations.

Today: The heart shape is a universally recognized symbol of love and affection.

| THINK HAPPY, BE HAPPY

CEREBRAL CAPACITY

If your brain were a digital video
recorder, it could hold three
million hours of TV shows.

| THINK HAPPY, BE HAPPY

HAPPINESS IN INTERNET TIME

6 a.m.: Emails sent early get read quickly.

8–9 a.m.: Tweets sent at this time are more positive, thanks to the refreshment of a good night's sleep.

8 p.m.: Facebook Likes increase as people hop online after dinner to see what their friends are up to.

ALL TIMES ARE BEAUTIFUL
FOR THOSE WHO MAINTAIN
JOY WITHIN THEM

TOP TEN "HAPPIEST" JOBS

1. Clergy
2. Firefighters
3. Physical therapists
4. Authors
5. Special education teachers
6. Teachers
7. Artists
8. Psychologists
9. Financial services sales agents
10. Operating engineers

COURAGE DOES NOT always ROAR

MARY ANNE RADMACHER

THE ORIGIN STORY

Was the high five invented by a professional baseball player in 1977 or by a college basketball team in 1979? Its exact origins are unclear, but by the 1980s this congratulatory gesture had become a staple of sports triumphs in America and around the globe. Today, the high five can celebrate anything from major milestones (SAT results or a baby's first steps) to the little things in life (a fixed flat tire or a yummy brownie).

IT'S NOT WHERE YOU TAKE THINGS FROM— IT'S WHERE YOU TAKE THEM TO.

HOW TO BLOW THE
PERFECT BUBBLEGUM BUBBLE

- Use more than one piece of gum for a bigger bubble.

- Choose gum with lots of sugar!

- Chew the gum for 5 minutes before blowing bubbles.

- Breathe in deeply to produce more air.

- Do what the pros do: Add peanut butter to your gum!

WISH SOMEONE HAPPY BIRTHDAY
IN MULTIPLE LANGUAGES

DUTCH: *Gelukkige Verjaardag!*

FARSI: *Tavalodet Mobârak!*

FRENCH: *Bon Anniversaire!*

GERMAN: *Alles Gute zum Geburtstag!*

GREEK: *Chronia Polla!*

ITALIAN: *Buon Compleanno!*

JAPANESE: *O tanjō-bi omedetōgozaimasu!*

RUSSIAN: *S dniom razhdjenia!*

SPANISH: *¡Feliz Cumpleaños!*

THAI: *Suk San Wan Keut!*

LIVE EVERY DAY

like it's YOUR

BIRTHDAY

The secret of love is in opening your heart

JAMES TAYLOR

BE·NICE
TO YOURSELF.
IT'S HARD
TO BE HAPPY
WHEN SOMEONE'S
MEAN TO YOU
ALL THE TIME.

POOL PARTY PLAYLIST

"Super Bass," Nicki Minaj

"Summer of '69," Bryan Adams

"Soak Up the Sun," Sheryl Crow

"Miami," Will Smith

"Good Vibrations," The Beach Boys

"Pumped Up Kicks," Foster the People

"Sweet Home Alabama," Lynyrd Skynyrd

"California Gurls," Katy Perry

JUST KEEP YOUR HEAD ABOVE,

SWIM

— JACK'S MANNEQUIN

TODAY WILL BE GREAT

SING IT IN THE SHOWER PLAYLIST

"Livin' on a Prayer," Bon Jovi

"Poker Face," Lady Gaga

"Brown Eyed Girl," Van Morrison

"It's Raining Men," The Weather Girls

"I Will Always Love You," Whitney Houston

"Don't Stop Believin'," Journey

"Smooth Criminal," Michael Jackson

"Think," Aretha Franklin

Let us be grateful to people who make us happy:
They are the charming gardeners who make our souls blossom.

—Marcel Proust

go
ahead,
make
my
day

A GOURMET PB&J, À LA RUTH REICHL

- Choose quality bread, such as Pullman or challah.

- Spread on sweet butter, then the peanut butter.

- Sprinkle on a little flaky salt.

- Go for strawberry jam, not jelly.

- Cut off the crusts.

- Microwave for 8 seconds to make it melty and delicious!

GREATEST LITERARY FRIENDSHIPS

Winnie-the-Pooh and Piglet, *Winnie-the-Pooh*

Harry Potter, Ron Weasley, and Hermione Granger,
Harry Potter series

Curious George and the Man in the Yellow Hat,
Curious George

Tom Sawyer and Huckleberry Finn,
The Adventures of Tom Sawyer/Huckleberry Finn

Dorothy, Scarecrow, Tin Man, and Cowardly Lion,
The Wonderful Wizard of Oz

Frodo Baggins and Samwise Gamgee, *The Lord of the Rings*

George Milton and Lennie Small, *Of Mice and Men*

Sherlock Holmes and Dr. John Watson, *Sherlock Holmes*

Anne Shirley and Diana Barry, *Anne of Green Gables*

The world is round so that friendship may encircle it.
— Pierre Teilhard de Chardin

The Best thing to Hold Onto in life is Each Other

Audrey Hepburn

YOU SEE THINGS AND YOU SAY *why?* BUT I DREAM THINGS THAT NEVER WERE; and I say WHY NOT?

George Bernard Shaw

SUNNIEST VACATION SPOTS

Alice Springs, Australia

Marseilles, France

Yuma, Arizona, USA

Lisbon, Portugal

Andalusia, Spain

Algeria, Africa

Rhodes Island, Greece

EVERYTHING YOU CAN IMAGINE IS REAL

PABLO PICASSO

HOW TO YODEL

Yodeling is singing while switching between your chest voice (the voice you use when you're comfortably singing low to medium notes that you're projecting from within your chest) and your head voice (used when you're singing high notes through your nasal cavity).

To practice, sing "yo-dah-lay-hee-hoo" in your chest voice. Then try changing a couple of the notes to your head voice, for example, just the "dah" and "hee." The basic yodeling format is singing low-low-low-high-high (the last high note is slightly lower than the first high note).

Watch out, Heidi—there's a new yodeler in town!

NEVER

GIVE

UP

NEVER

SURRENDER

GALAXY QUEST

WHIMSICAL BUTTERFLY NAMES

Mustard White

Ruddy Hairstreak

Sleepy Duskywing

California Dogface

Mormon Metalmark

Blue-Eyed Sailor

Pale Cracker

Confused Cloudywing

Malicious Skipper

Frosted Elfin

DO
HOPE
OF WHAT MAKES YOU
HAPPY

WORK FOR SOMETHING BECAUSE IT
IS GOOD, NOT JUST BECAUSE IT
STANDS A CHANCE TO SUCCEED

Vaclav Havel

EVOCATIVE OYSTER NAMES

FRENCH KISS: Neguac, New Brunswick

HAMA HAMA: Hood Canal, Washington

FANNY BAY: Baynes Sound, British Columbia

NAKED COWBOY: Long Island Sound, New York

PUGWASH: Pugwash Point, Nova Scotia

BEAVERTAIL: Narragansett Bay, Rhode Island

SHINNECOCK: Shinnecock Bay, New York

EFFINGHAM: Barkley Sound, Vancouver

RAM ISLAND: Long Island Sound, Connecticut

HOOTENANNY: Hood Canal, Washington

the WORLD *is your* OYSTER

THE WORLD'S OLDEST OPERATING ROLLER COASTERS

Leap-the-Dips (1902)—Altoona, Pennsylvania

Scenic Railway (1912)—Melbourne, Australia

Rutschebanen (1914)—Copenhagen, Denmark

Wild One (1917)—Hull, Massachusetts,
then Upper Marlboro, Maryland

Jack Rabbit (1920)—Rochester, New York

Jack Rabbit (1920)—West Mifflin, Pennsylvania

Roller Coaster (1921)—Farmington, Utah

Hullamvasut (1922)—Budapest, Hungary

Big Dipper (1923)—Blackpool Pleasure Beach, England

Thunderhawk (1923)—Allentown, Pennsylvania

My candle burns at both ends;
It will not last the night;
But ah, my foes
&
oh my friends—
it gives a lovely light.

EDNA ST. VINCENT MILLAY

| THINK HAPPY, BE HAPPY

keep a green tree
in your heart
& perhaps the singing
bird will
come

- chinese proverb

CHILL-OUT PLAYLIST

"Across the Universe," The Beatles

"The Wind," Cat Stevens

"I Will Follow You Into The Dark," Death Cab for Cutie

"Your Song," Ellie Goulding

"Sympathy," Goo Goo Dolls

"Hallelujah," Jeff Buckley

"Banana Pancakes," Jack Johnson

"Turning Tables," Adele

2 BLESSED 2 BE STRESSED

Whatever it is... It's probably not that important.

THE LARGEST LIBRARY IN THE WORLD

The U.S. Library of Congress has approximately 838 miles of bookshelves, more than 35 million books, 3.4 million recordings, 13.6 million photographs, 5.4 million maps, 6.5 million pieces of sheet music, and 68 million manuscripts—all ready to be explored.

Tomorrow is fresh with no mistakes in it.

—Lucy Maud Montgomery

ROASTY TOASTY PUMPKIN SEEDS

Serves 4

Ingredients:
1½ cups raw whole pumpkin seeds
2 teaspoons melted butter
Salt to taste

Preheat oven to 300°F. Toss the seeds in a bowl with the melted butter and a pinch of salt. Spread the seeds on a baking sheet and bake for about 45 minutes, stirring occasionally, until golden brown.

DON'T JUDGE EACH DAY BY THE HARVEST YOU REAP, BUT BY THE SEEDS YOU PLANT

IF THE WIND WILL NOT SERVE, TAKE TO THE OARS

—LATIN PROVERB

BIRDS THAT MATE FOR LIFE

Bald eagle

Laysan albatross

Mute swan

Scarlet macaw

Whooping crane

California condor

Atlantic puffin

WHY FIT IN WHEN YOU WERE BORN TO

STAND OUT?

-Dr. Seuss

WATERMELON MINT ICE POPS

Ingredients:
4 cups seedless watermelon, cut into 1-inch pieces
2 tablespoons sugar
¼ cup mint leaves, minced
2 teaspoons finely grated lemon zest
pinch of salt

Puree the watermelon with the sugar in a blender until smooth. Mix in the mint, lemon zest, and salt. Pour the mixture into 8 ice-pop molds or 2 standard ice cube trays (insert ice-pop sticks before ice pops are completely frozen), and freeze until hard, about 3 hours.

I MAKE my OWN SUNSHINE!

—Alyssa Bonagura

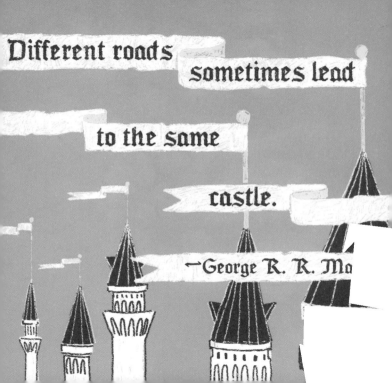

Different roads sometimes lead to the same castle.

—George R. R. Ma

MOST POPULAR CRAYOLA CRAYON COLORS
(and when they made it into the pack)

Blue (1903)

Cerulean (1990)

Purple Heart (1997)

Midnight Blue (1958)

Aquamarine (1957)

Caribbean Green (1998)

Periwinkle (1949)

Denim (1993)

Cerise (1993)

Blizzard Blue (1972)

| THINK HAPPY, BE HAPPY

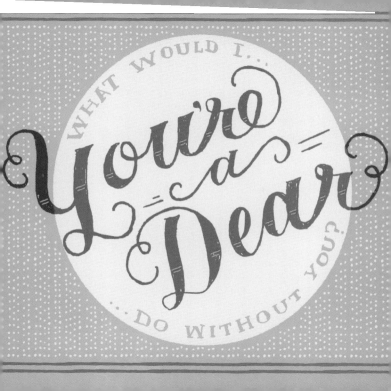

A HAPPY WORKOUT!

A study was conducted at Vanderbilt University measuring the amount of calories expended in laughing. It turned out that 10 to 15 minutes of genuine laughter burned up to 50 calories. That means that if you laugh for 10 to 15 minutes a day, you could burn enough calories to lose 4.4 pounds in a year!

I Love Myself when I am Laughing

ZORA NEALE HURSTON

it's always too early to quit

CHEWY CHOCOLATY TRAIL MIX

Ingredients:
1 cup diced dried fruit of your choice
½ cup raisins, dried cherries, or cranberries
1½ cups unsalted sunflower seeds
1 cup peanuts, walnuts, or almonds
½ cup M&M's or Reese's Pieces

Mix together and enjoy the next time you hit the trail or need an energy boost!

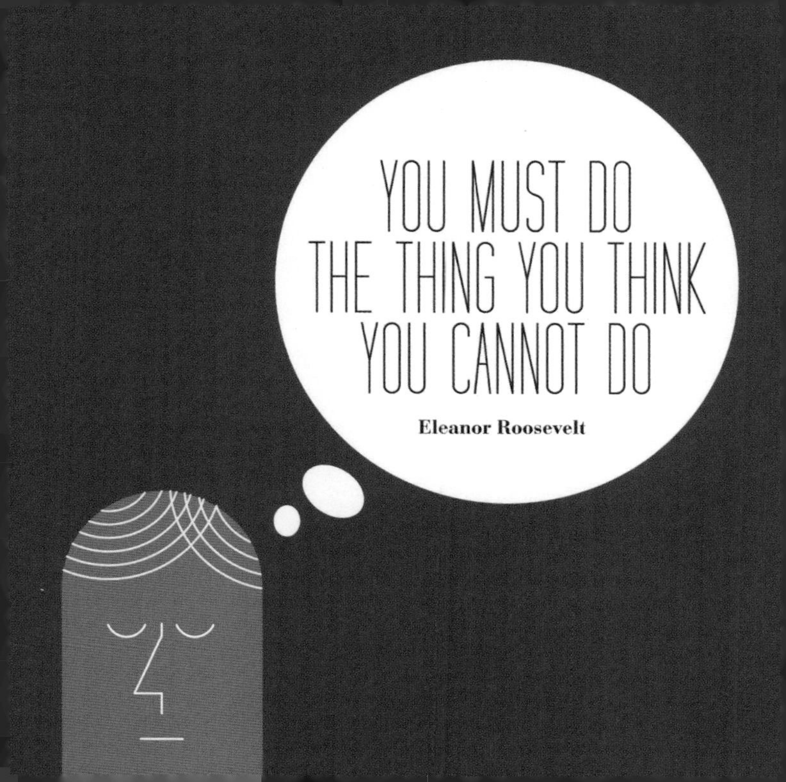
YOU MUST DO
THE THING YOU THINK
YOU CANNOT DO
Eleanor Roosevelt

MOST BEAUTIFUL BRIDGES IN THE WORLD

Golden Gate Bridge; San Francisco, California, USA

Tower Bridge; London, England, UK

Brooklyn Bridge; New York City, New York, USA

Chengyang Wind and Rain Bridge; Sanjiang, China

Ponte Vecchio; Florence, Italy

West Montrose Covered Bridge; Ontario, Canada

Iron Bridge; Shropshire, England, UK

Bridge of Sighs; Venice, Italy

Pont du Gard; Nîmes, France

Khaju Bridge; Isfahan, Iran

Do all Things with Love

A HAPPY FACT

Scientists have found that daydreaming increases our creativity and ability to create solutions and ideas. That's good news, because we daydream approximately 47 percent of our waking hours!

If not us, WHO? If not now, WHEN?

PASSION FRUIT DAIQUIRI

Serves 4

Ingredients:
¾ cup frozen or bottled passion fruit juice,
or 15 passion fruits
⅓ cup light rum
6 firmly packed tablespoons light brown sugar
3 cups crushed ice

1. If using frozen or bottled passion fruit juice,
proceed to Step 2. If using fresh fruits, cut them in
half and scrape out the pulp. Force the pulp through
a strainer; you should have about ¾ cup of juice.

2. Combine the passion fruit juice, rum, and brown
sugar in a blender with the ice and process until
smooth. Pour into martini glasses and serve
immediately.

you are my SUNSHINE

OLIVER HOOD

IN EVERY REAL MAN A CHILD IS HIDDEN THAT WANTS TO PLAY.
— FRIEDRICH NIETZSCHE

SLEEPY-TIME PLAYLIST

"Love and Some Verses," Iron & Wine

"The Fear You Won't Fall," Joshua Radin

"Free Fallin'," John Mayer

"Vienna," Billy Joel

"Falling in Love at a Coffee Shop," Landon Pigg

"Beach Baby," Bon Iver

"Falling Slowly," Glen Hansard and Marketa Irglova

THERE IS nothing that cannot happen today.

- Mark Twain

HOW TO TOAST IN DIFFERENT LANGUAGES

Arabic (Egyptian): *Fisehatak* (fee-sa-HA-tak)

Bulgarian: *Na zdrave* (NAZ-dra-vey)

Chinese (Mandarin): *Gan bei* (gan BAY)

French: *À votre santé* (ah VOH-truh sahn-TAY)

German: *Prost* (pROHST)

Hebrew: *L' chaim* (le CHY-em)

Italian: *Salute* (sah-LOO-teh)

Japanese: *Kanpai* (kam-PIE)

Polish: *Na zdrowie* (naz-DROH-vee-ay)

Spanish: *Salud* (sah-LUD)

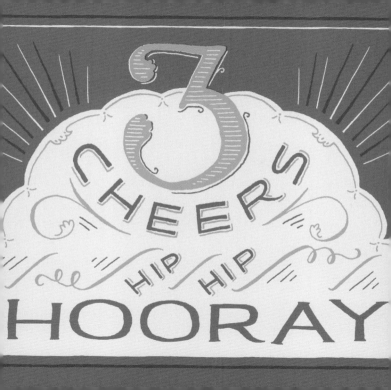

THE WORLD'S MOST ROMANTIC CITIES

Paris, France

Monte Carlo, Monaco

Lisbon, Portugal

Jaipur, India

Fez, Morocco

Bruges, Belgium

Kyoto, Japan

Florence, Italy

Barcelona, Spain

Venice, Italy

HAVE PATIENCE
WITH ALL
THINGS,

BUT FIRST OF
ALL, YOURSELF

St. Francis de Sales

BEST STARGAZING
LOCATIONS ON EARTH

Wiruna, New South Wales, Australia

Hawaii, USA

Valentia Island, Ireland

Southern Africa

Atacama Desert, Chile

Joshua Tree National Park, California, USA

Mont-Mégantic National Park, Quebec, Canada

I LOVE YOU
more than
ALL THE STARS

Be YOURSELF. Everyone else is taken.

OSCAR WILDE

RAINY DAY PLAYLIST

"Me and You," Nero

"Seven (The Twelves Remix)," Fever Ray

"Groove Is in the Heart," Deee-Lite

"Only Happy When It Rains," Garbage

"The Difficult Kind," Sheryl Crow

"Rainy Day, Dream Away," Jimi Hendrix

"After the Dance," Marvin Gaye

"Thief in the Night," The Rolling Stones

"Blue Eyes Crying in the Rain," Willie Nelson

THROWBACK: '60S SLANG

A gas: A lot of fun

Beat feet: Leave the area quickly

Bummed out: Depressed

Decked out: All dressed up

Dig: Understand

Fuzz: The police

Hairy: Out of control

Later: Good-bye

Pig out: Overeat

Shades: Sunglasses

MUST-HAVE ALBUMS TO
START A RECORD COLLECTION

Abbey Road—The Beatles

Tommy—The Who

Experience—Jimi Hendrix

Thriller—Michael Jackson

Horses—Patti Smith

Goodbye Yellow Brick Road—Elton John

Blood on the Tracks—Bob Dylan

Greatest Hits—The Supremes

Born to Run—Bruce Springsteen

London Calling—The Clash

IS LIFE NOT A THOUSAND TIMES TOO SHORT FOR US TO BORE OURSELVES?
- FRIEDRICH NIETZSCHE

GO INTO THE world and DO **WELL.** GO MORE IMPORTANTLY, INTO THE world and DO **GOOD.**

-Minor Myers

CLASSIC ADVENTURE NOVELS

The Call of the Wild—Jack London

The Odyssey—Homer

Hatchet—Gary Paulsen

Moby-Dick—Herman Melville

Jurassic Park—Michael Crichton

Around the World in Eighty Days—Jules Verne

The Three Musketeers—Alexandre Dumas

Treasure Island—Robert Louis Stevenson

Alice's Adventures in Wonderland—Lewis Carroll

Gulliver's Travels—Jonathan Swift

TO LIVE
will be an

awfully

BIG

adventure

J. M. Barrie
PETER PAN

HOW TO BREW THE
PERFECT CUP OF TEA

1. Add boiling water to a tea bag in a mug and steep for two minutes.

2. Remove the bag and add milk. Let cool for six minutes until it reaches the optimal temperature of 140°F.

3. Don't let it sit for longer than 17 minutes and 30 seconds, or the tea will be past its best.

For Fast-Acting Relief try Slowing down.

—Lily Tomlin

STRONG TREES
FOR CLIMBING

Kumquat

Loquat

Oak

Woody wattle

Apple

Mulberry

PERFECTLY SIMPLE LEMONADE

Serves 4

Ingredients:

1 cup sugar
1 cup water

1 cup freshly squeezed lemon juice
3 to 4 cups cold water

1. Make simple syrup by heating the sugar and water in a small saucepan until the sugar is dissolved completely.

2. Extract the juice from 4 to 6 lemons, enough for one cup of juice. You can leave some pulp in, but make sure the seeds are removed.

3. Pour the juice and sugar water into a pitcher. Add the cold water, more or less to the desired strength. Refrigerate 30 to 40 minutes. If the lemonade is a little sweet for your taste, add a little more straight lemon juice to it.

Live simply

so that others may

simply live

AND DELIGHT REIGNED.

FRANCES HODGSON BURNETT

HAPPINESS = HEALTH

Happy people are less likely to send out surges of stress hormones that contribute to heart disease. On the other hand, chronically unhappy people often have increased blood pressure and decreased immunity.

A Light Heart Lives Long

William Shakespeare

I have LOVED THE STARS TOO FONDLY Fearful TO·BE OF THE NIGHT

– SARAH WILLIAMS

LIVE A LITTLE

MAKE THE MOST OF A PHOTOBOOTH

1. Fake a fistfight with your friend.

2. Seduce the camera.

3. Pretend you're on a roller coaster.

4. Have a dance party.

5. Look surprised.

6. Blow a kiss.

7. Shush your friend.

8. Give yourself a mustache with your (long) hair.

9. Put something silly on your head.

10. Show your friend the (muscle-y) way to the beach.

Learn from yesterday,
Live for today,
Hope for tomorrow.
-Albert Einstein

HEALTH, CONTENTMENT, AND TRUST ARE YOUR GREATEST POSSESSIONS, AND FREEDOM YOUR GREATEST JOY

Buddha

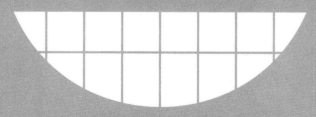

AN

ADVENTURE

IS ONLY AN

INCONVENIENCE

RIGHTLY CONSIDERED.

GILBERT K. CHESTERTON

GOOD MORNING PLAYLIST

"Here Comes the Sun," The Beatles

"Daylight," Matt & Kim

"I Can See Clearly Now," Johnny Nash

"Wake Me Up Before You Go-Go," Wham!

"Wide Awake," Katy Perry

"Walking on Sunshine," Katrina and the Waves

"New Soul," Yael Naim

"First Day of My Life," Bright Eyes

Don't Let yesterday use up too much of Today

Will Rogers

BOWL LIKE A PRO!

- Keep your wrist firm with the thumb that's inside the ball pointing to 10 or 11 o'clock

- Relax your hand's grip on the ball

- Square your hips to the line during delivery

- Keep the elbow on your ball hand close to your body

- Bend your knee on your last step before you roll

EVERYTHING WILL BOWL OVER

GO NUTS

Squirrels forgetting where
they put their acorns results in
thousands of new trees each year.

GREAT OAKS FROM LITTLE acorns GROW

| THINK HAPPY, BE HAPPY

YOUR TIME IS *LIMITED* SO DON'T *waste it* LIVING SOMEONE ELSE'S LIFE

STEVE JOBS

MAKE YOUR OWN
LAVENDER HOME SPRAY

Ingredients:
1 teaspoon lavender essential oil
3½ cups filtered water

Pour the filtered water into an empty spray
bottle. Add the lavender oil and shake well.

Anyone who keeps
the ability to
see beauty never
grows old.
– Franz Kafka

TOGETHER FOREVER

Gene Cernan, the last man to walk on the moon, promised his daughter he'd do something special for her: He'd write her initials on the moon. He did, and her initials, TDC, will probably be on the moon for over 50,000 years.

DECIPHER YOUR DOODLES

FACES: Indicate your current mood

FLOWERS: Rounded petals suggest a family-centric person. Doodling a bunch of flowers means you're sociable.

HEARTS: You're a romantic, of course!

INTRICATE PATTERNS: Can indicate an introverted or obsessive personality

STAIRS AND LADDERS: Symbols of ambition or desire

STARS: Show optimism

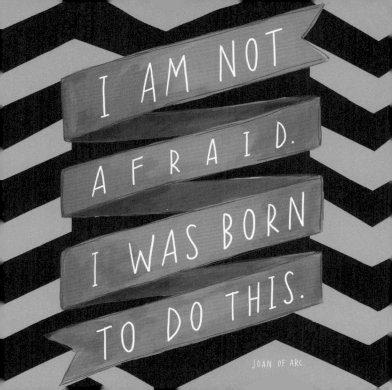

I AM NOT AFRAID. I WAS BORN TO DO THIS.

JOAN OF ARC

EASY AS APPLE PIE

Serves 4-6

Ingredients:

2 pie crusts
3-4 medium apples, peeled, cored, and sliced
1 cup sugar
¼ teaspoon nutmeg
½ stick unsalted butter, cut into bits

Preheat oven to 375°F. Place one of the pie crusts in a pie pan. Add apples and sprinkle with sugar and nutmeg. Top with butter, place the remaining crust over the top, and press to seal. Cut a few slits into the dough to let steam escape. Bake until golden brown, 1 hour.

IF YOU WISH TO MAKE AN APPLE PIE FROM SCRATCH,
YOU MUST FIRST INVENT THE UNIVERSE. -CARL SAGAN

LIVE YOUR QUESTIONS
NOW, AND PERHAPS
EVEN WITHOUT KNOWING
IT, YOU WILL LIVE
ALONG SOME DISTANT
DAY INTO YOUR ANSWERS

Rainer Maria Rilke

SOME DAYS ALL I DO IS WATCH THE SKY

— SOMETHING CORPORATE

FEARLESS PLAYLIST

"Survivor," Destiny's Child

"Broken," Antigone Rising

"Just Stand Up," R&B Divas United

"Live Like We're Dying," Kris Allen

"Be Calm," fun.

"Stand," Lenny Kravitz

"Just Say Yes," Snow Patrol

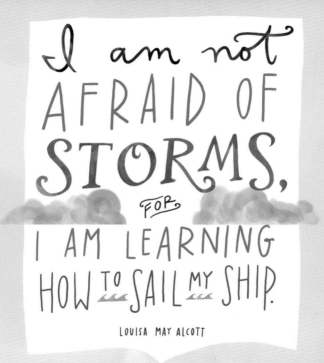

I am not AFRAID OF STORMS, FOR I AM LEARNING HOW TO SAIL MY SHIP.

LOUISA MAY ALCOTT

I destroy my ENEMIES when I make them my FRIENDS.

ABRAHAM LINCOLN

HONEY OAT GRANOLA BARS

Makes 18 bars

Ingredients:

4½ cups rolled oats
1 cup all-purpose flour
1 teaspoon baking soda
1 teaspoon vanilla extract
⅔ cup butter, softened

½ cup honey
⅓ cup packed brown sugar
2 cups miniature semisweet chocolate chips

Preheat oven to 325°F. Combine all ingredients in a bowl, stirring in chocolate chips last. Press mixture into lightly greased 13- by 9-inch pan. Bake for 18 to 22 minutes or until golden brown. Let cool for 10 minutes, then cut into bars.

Tip: Add extra honey to avoid crumbly bars!

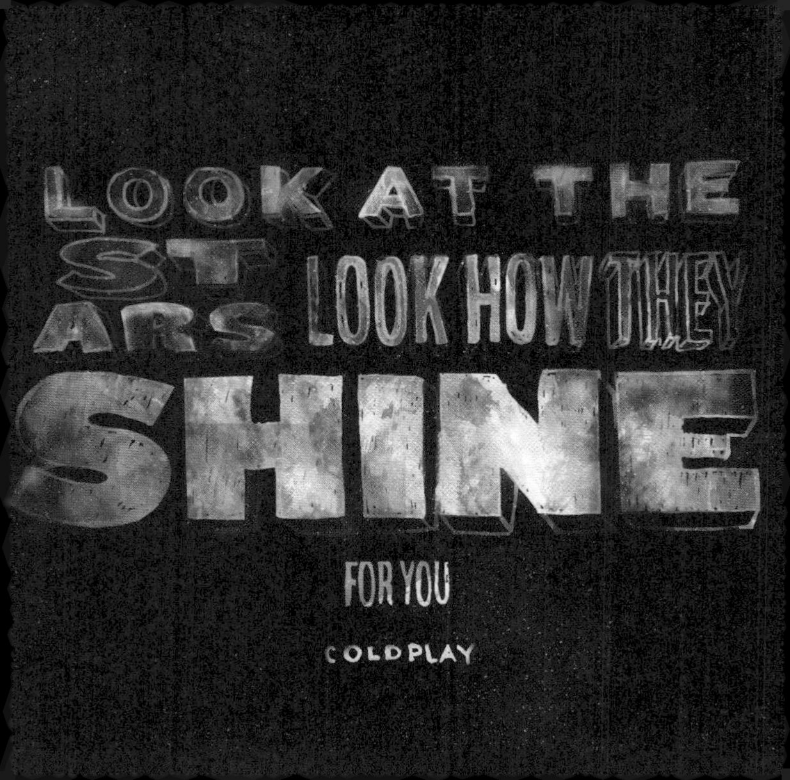
LOOK AT THE
STARS
LOOK HOW THEY
SHINE
FOR YOU
COLDPLAY

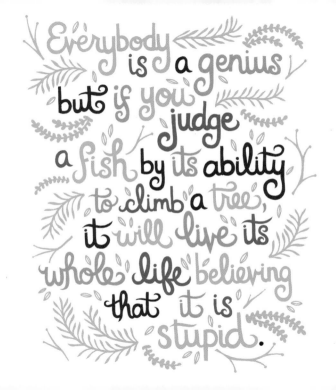

HOW TO FROST A CAKE PERFECTLY

- Make sure the cake is fully cooked; an inserted toothpick should come out clean.

- Allow the cake to cool completely.

- Lay the frosting on instead of rubbing it on.

- Use a spatula or knife to level the frosting.

- Lay a piece of parchment paper on the cake. Use your finger to lightly smooth the icing, then gently peel the paper away.

Don't let 1 cloud obliterate the whole sky.

—ANAÏS NIN

Today is our GREATEST adventure

BEST SPORTS COMEBACKS

1. Buffalo Bills (vs. Houston Oilers)
NFL playoffs, 1993

2. Boston Red Sox (vs. New York Yankees)
MLB championships, 2004

3. Illinois Fighting Illini (vs. Arizona Wildcats)
NCAA basketball regional final, 2005

4. Gary Player
The Masters (golf), 1978

5. Michigan State Spartans (vs. Northwestern Wildcats)
NCAA football, 2006

NEVER
confuse a
SINGLE DEFEAT
with a
FINAL DEFEAT.

F. SCOTT FITZGERALD

THERE IS NOTHING STRONGER IN THE WORLD THAN GENTLENESS.

Han Suyin

BEST FAMILY DOGS

Bulldog

Beagle

Bull Terrier

Collie

Newfoundland

Vizsla

Irish Setter

Poodle

Labrador Retriever

Golden Retriever

Mutt

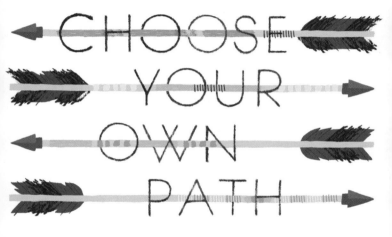

CHOOSE YOUR OWN PATH

| THINK HAPPY, BE HAPPY

BLACKBERRY SMOOTHIE

Serves 2

Ingredients:

1 banana
2 cups (packed) spinach leaves
1 cup frozen blackberries
1 cup nonfat yogurt
½ cup fresh orange juice
1 teaspoon finely grated peeled ginger
1 teaspoon honey or light agave syrup (nectar)

Blend all ingredients in a blender until smooth.
Divide between two glasses; serve mmediately.

All good things are Wild & Free

—HENRY DAVID THOREAU

HOW DID THE DOUGHNUT GET ITS HOLE?

According to one tale, Captain Hanson Gregory, a 19th-century Maine sea captain, was eating a cake while sailing through a storm. Suddenly, the ship rocked violently and threw him against the ship's wheel, impaling his cake on one of its spokes. Seeing how well the spoke held his cake, Gregory began ordering all of his cakes with holes in them.

Friendship is a single soul dwelling in two bodies.

— Aristotle

wherever
you go,
whatever
you do,
be in love!

~Rumi

CLOSE YOUR EYES

AND YOU CAN FLY

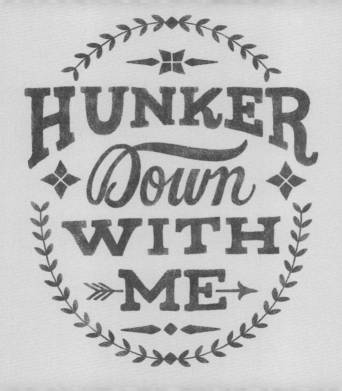

HUNKER Down WITH ME

SLEEP AWAY YOUR STRESS

Stress and anxiety are the result of cortisol being
produced in the adrenal glands. By releasing the
antidote (growth hormone), a nap can reduce that
stress and anxiety and make you a calmer person.
So don't worry, start napping.

Nothing a Nap Can't Fix

Life is just a Bowl of Cherries

—Lew Brown & Buddy DeSylva

ACTION IS CHARACTER

F. SCOTT FITZGERALD

DO YOU FULLY EXHALE?

Most people inhale much more fully than they
exhale, which can elevate the amount of oxygen
in the body. Even just a little extra cxygen can
explain episodes of dizziness, blurry vision, or
light-headedness. So let it out!

BE GLAD OF LIFE BECAUSE
IT GIVES YOU THE CHANCE
TO LOVE AND TO WORK
AND TO PLAY AND TO LOOK
UP AT THE STARS

Henry Van Dyke

THREE-STEP SUGAR COOKIES

Makes 4 dozen

Ingredients:

2¾ cups all-purpose flour

1 teaspoon baking soda

½ teaspoon baking powder

¼ teaspoon salt

1 cup unsalted butter, softened

1½ cups white sugar

1 egg

1 teaspoon vanilla extract

Preheat oven to 375°F. In a small bowl, stir together the flour, baking soda, baking powder, and salt, then set aside.

In a large bowl, cream the butter and sugar together until smooth. Beat in the egg and vanilla, then gradually blend in the dry ingredients. Roll the dough into 1-inch balls and place, spaced out, on ungreased cookie sheets.

Bake 8 to 10 minutes or until golden. Let stand two minutes, then place on wire racks to cool.

HAPPINESS IS HOMEMADE

BIRD CALLS THAT SOUND LIKE WORDS

BARRED OWL: "Who cooks for you?
Who cooks for you all?"

RED-EYED VIREO: "Look up! See me: Over here,
this way. Do you hear me? Higher still, chewy!"

CHESTNUT-SIDED WARBLER:
"Very, very pleased to meetcha!"

EASTERN MEADOWLARK: "Spring of the year!
See you, soon. I will see you. Spring is here!"

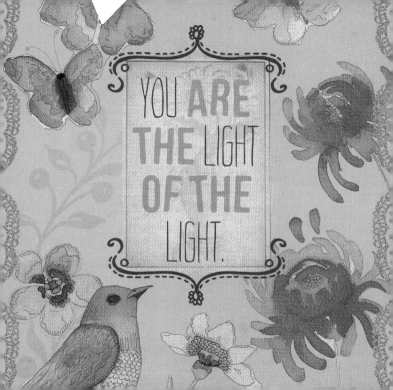

YOU ARE
THE LIGHT
OF THE
LIGHT.

| THINK HAPPY, BE HAPPY

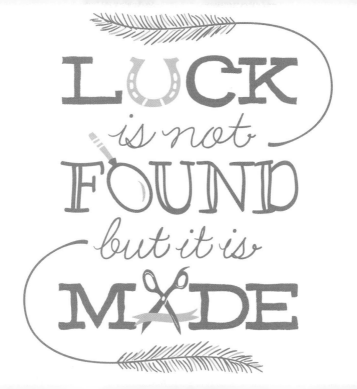

ON TOP OF EVERY
MOUNTAIN
there was a great
LONGING FOR ANOTHER
even higher
MOUNTAIN
-DIRTY PROJECTORS

Tomorrow TO FRESH WOODS and PASTURES NEW

JOHN MILTON

PLANTS THAT FLOWER YEAR-ROUND

Peace Lily

Lantana

African Iris

Wedelia

African Daisy

DEEP IN · THEIR ROOTS, ALL FLOWERS KEEP THE LIGHT. —Theodore Roethke

MOST FOLKS ARE ABOUT AS HAPPY AS THEY MAKE UP THEIR Minds to BE

Abraham Lincoln

"SAY CHEESE!" AROUND THE WORLD

Spain: *Whiskey*

Portugal: *X* (pronounced "sheez")

France: *Ouistiti* (translation: marmoset)

Germany: *Lächeln* (translation: smile)

China: *Qiézi* (translation: eggplant)

Denmark: *Appelsin* (translation: orange)

Korea: *Kimchi* (translation: Korean pickle or side dish)

Russia: *Seer* (translation: cheese)

Sweden: *Omelett* (translation: omelet)

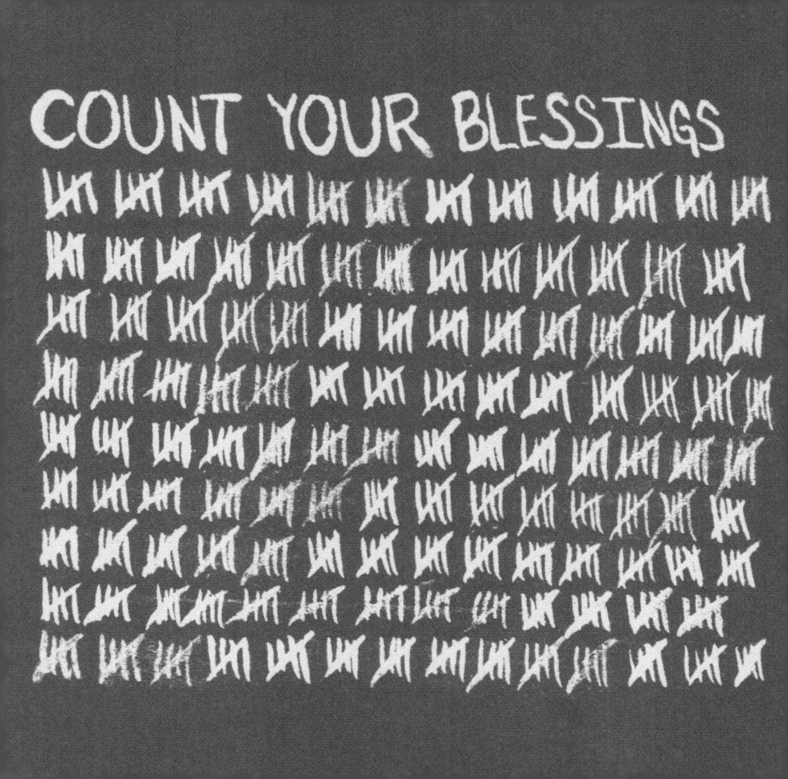
COUNT YOUR BLESSINGS

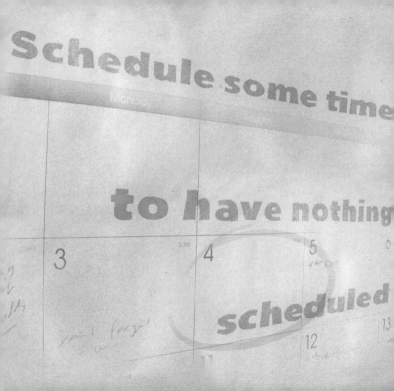

STYLE ICONS

Marilyn Monroe

Grace Jones

Elizabeth Taylor

Grace Kelly

Chloë Sevigny

Katharine Hepburn

Brigitte Bardot

Frida Kahlo

Sophia Loren

Jackie O

The Loving are the Daring

—Bayard Taylor

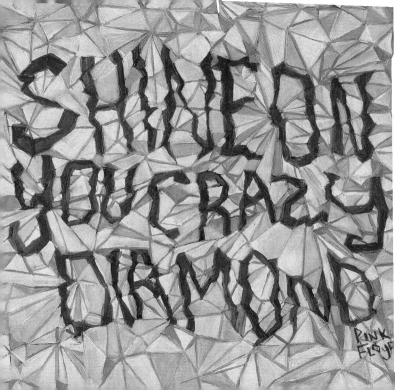

never stop

IMAGE CREDITS

IMAGE CREDITS (continued)

SOURCE LIST

p. 12   pbs.org

p. 16   scientificamerican.com

p. 20   online.wsj.com

p. 22   forbes.com

p. 28   *The Book of Nice*
        by Josh Chetwynd

p. 36   leewardlaw.com

p. 60   gilttaste.com

p. 78   thetravelerszone.com

p. 84   ehow.com

p. 106 latimes.com

p. 122 loc.gov

p. 138 audubon.org

p. 144 foodandwine.com

p. 148 sensationalcolor.com

p. 152 mc.vanderbilt.edu

p. 162 neatorama.com

p. 168 newyorker.com

p. 172 *The Barbecue! Bible*
        by Steven Raichlen

p. 190 buzzfeed.com

p. 196 ratestogo.com

p. 206 the60sofficialsite.com

p. 222 telegraph.co.uk

p. 234 howstuffworks.com

p. 256 epicbowling.com

p. 270 nationalaviation.org

p. 302 giverslog.com

p. 310 askmen.com

p. 316 cesarsway.com

p. 326 gather.com

p. 336 *Take a Nap! Change Your life*
        by Sara C. Mednick

p. 344 *The Miracle Ball Method*
        by Elaine Petrone

p. 362 *My First Bird Book and Bird
        Feeder* by Sharon Lovejoy

p. 370 gardenguides.com